Legacy.

Rochelle Brown

BookLeaf
Publishing

India | USA | UK

Legacy. © 2024 Rochelle Brown

All rights reserved.

Presentation by *BookLeaf Publishing*

Web: www.bookleafpub.com

E-mail: info@bookleafpub.com

ISBN: 9789358313444

First edition 2024

DEDICATION

Evelyn,

Before you I didn't know myself.

I love you yesterday, today, tomorrow and always.

Mama x

Until

Love was passion. Love was a fire ignited by touch and fierce emotion and heightened only by ever growing closeness. It was uncertainty and risks unknown; a fever of beating hearts and fights followed by tears and break ups then dates and make ups.

Until you. A gentle warm kiss from the sun. A consistency I'd never dreamed of. Your tiny hands on my mountain of a body.
Your eyes that know nothing but me. I am your constant and I will always be your constant. In a world where everything is moving, you stand still, protected on a pedestal of love.

Until you I never knew how calm love could be.

Until you I wasn't me.

Bubbles

My skin is peppered with bubbles and tingling
from the hot water.

It's been days; I couldn't say how long.

Last night you were poorly and thought I ached
from the long day your solemn face haunted my
mind. The boilers too noisy. The water splashing
will keep you up. I can shower in the morning.

I don't shower in the morning.

We wake to the sound of your rattling coughand
I pull you closer and tell you it's going to be ok
even though I don't know if it will be and you
don't know what I'm saying. Breathe.

I pull on your clothes and try and get ready
myself but you need me and I hold you so I'm
not feeling my best as I drop you off and set off
to work.

Tonight you fall asleep covered in comfort in
your fathers arms. I tiptoe into the bathroom. My

skin peppered with bubbles and tingling from
the hot water.

It's been days; I couldn't say how long.

Waves

My memories are dimly lit.

They are faint pictures from the light of my
phone or the flashing of the muted television.

They are littered with the background noise of
hairdryers and oceans or whichever white noise I
could get my hands on.

Your tiny chest rising and falling like the tide.
I'm fixated; I watch it for minutes before I allow
myself to drift away.

Then the crash of the waves jolts me awake.

We are stranded on our own deserted island,
there is no respite but there's so much joy
between the crashes.

I'm with you but I am completely alone.

I'm with you and I am whole.

Giving

Motherhood is not giving birth.

It's giving everything.
It's giving up a sense of self in place of a
responsibility.
It's giving in to late nights and early mornings.
It's giving your all to make yourself a home that
keeps her safe.
It's giving your time and energy to a little soul
who's figuring out the world.
It's giving thanks to the little moments in
between the chaos.
It's giving yourself a break in ways that used to
be a chore.
It's not giving up when the days are long.
It not giving in when your body is aching and
you feel like you're carrying the weight of
someone else's world on your shoulders.
Motherhood is giving your heart to one you have
grown and giving your life in order for them to
have a better one.

Masterpiece

I have to pinch myself sometimes to remind me
that this is real.
Your soft translucent skin that graces your your
body isn't a dream and I created you. I protected
you for nine months and continued to long after
you entered this world. I made your laugh and
made you laugh and I hold you close, my
precious baby, as life unfolds in front of us.
With each heartbeat, a melody of love fills me
up in a symphony.
You are a canvas of every good feeling I've ever
felt. You are a masterpiece. I marvel at the very
existence of you.

Daddy

Your daddy is gentle, kind and warm,
He loves quietly but with ease,
His fingertips hold a thousand stories,
A sanctuary that never flees.

He paints the world in hues of joy,
An anchor in life's maze,
A mirror of all of the good that you do
In the middle of mundane haze.

Your daddy would move oceans,
To be in the presence of your laugh,
He'd move mountains to catch a glimpse of your
smile,
And take all the tears on your behalf.

Your daddy is a quiet man,
But in the presence of his calm,
Is all the love you could ever need,
Carried softly in his arms.

Shelter

"Take one" I say though I have but one piece
left.
And although shadows conspire I dig deep and
find another. It's not much but it's enough for
you.

A weathered oak and evergreen, we stand side
by side in our valley.
We climb, we continue, we grow. I'm steady
while you shoot. My roots are anchored deep.

My soil is your foundation and I nourish the
ground around you.
It's silent resilience. A forest of nurture paving
the way for young seedlings.

We stand tall together. We are an orchard of
strength in the winds of change.
The rings our scars, the bark our skin, the
weather our challenges. I shelter you.

Unconditional

I want your days to be long but feel short from the fun that you are having.
I hope that you look back on your childhood and know that there was love wrapped around even the most mundane activities.
I need you to know that my love for you surpasses anything I could have ever dreamed or imagined.
I believe that there is magic in everything you think and do and your potential is more than the boxes people will try and put you in.
I want hope need and believe you were put on this earth to show me the power of unconditional love.

Memories

I want to rewind I want go back,
I want to give me all the things that I lacked.

I want to hold you for the first time again, and
feel that warmth in our own little den.

I want to see the rows and rows of white,
on the line outside as the day got bright.

I want to hold your tiny hand in mine,
I want to tell me that it's all going to be fine.

I want to relive all the things that we've done,
I want relove you but it's already gone.

But if I could turn back time I wouldn't go,
I'd miss the you that you are and I'd miss you
so.

Mama

Your chubby cheeks pressed close against mine
make my heart flutter, you are nothing like I've
ever held or felt before.
Other babies have passed my arms but the love I
feel for you is like no other.
Your big blue eyes lighting up when I enter a
room make me feel invincible. I am yours. I am
only yours in that moment and I am important,
even if it is just to you.
I am mama. I am ruler of your whole universe. I
am the reason your day can be good or bad.
You are baba. You are a tiny human grasping at
what little skills you've learnt from me and
making sense of the world in front of you.
Together we are one. Together we can mould a
path for you to take. Together we can do
anything.

Here

You are you.
You are "so well behaved"
You are "really coming on with your eating"
You are "starting to count to five"
And I am me. I am working. I am missing you
learning and I am terrified.
That you will only know me from 6pm. And
starting at half past five.
But I am there sweet baby.
I am asking how you are doing. I am calling to
see how you are.
I am trying to make money so weekends seem
funny with your brother and daddy and I.
I am missing you walk and I'm missing you talk
but sweet baby I know you do I.
I am there in the night inbetween nightmares and
dreams armed with kisses and love.
I am there to teach you how to put on your
shoes, and to count five seconds until I run and
give you tickles.
I am there to see how well behaved you are
queuing patiently for nursery.
I am there in the quiet moments, arming you
with everything, sacrificing time to give you the
quality of it.
I am me and I am trying the best way I can be.

Daisy

I feel you in spotting the first winter robin
When the autumn wind tickles my skin.
I feel you in daisies, I feel you in the days
breeze,
I know that I felt you within.

It wasn't your time and I say that I am fine,
But I know you once existed in me,
Energy cannot be destroyed so I'll carry on this
void,
Won't be told that feeling sad is silly.

Because I won't get to tickle or hear your giggle,
Or know what voice sounds like
But in my head is the life that you led
If only it had been your time.

No headstone, no grave, just move on be brave
Your life three months in my tummy
And while out here your name is not clear,
I will still always be your mummy.

Honour

What an honour it is to be your mummy,
To hold you every day.
What a pleasure it is to hold your hand and
watch over you as you play.
What a treasure you are to be with as you
explore the world around.
What a joy it is to share your life and turn
around your frown
What a great feeling it is to know that I will be
your forever friend,
What an honour it is to be your mummy until the
very end.

Time

One day you're a tiny beating heart,
The next you're in my arms.
The days are long, the years are short,
Today is manic, my memories calm.

I wish the day away to bed,
I miss you when you're asleep,
I'm treasuring every single second,
Praying for the next leap.

I watch in awe as you take your first steps,
I'm nervous to see you go.
One day you're a tiny baby,
The next I wish it would slow.

I'm ironing tiny school shirts,
I'm fumbling for clean socks.
I hope your happy, I hope your kind
I hope you're not put into a box.

One day you're a child still need your mama,
And one day you will be grown.
But whatever happens my dear baby,
You will never be alone.

Seasons

You're in the spring of your life. Everything is new. It's blooming and sprouting and green and fresh, like you.

You wait for the summer like you wait for Christmas. Eagerly and wanting in complete blissful ignorance of the world around you.

I am in summer. You chase its warmth and envy its long days but dear I wish you would cherish the spring.

For once you are in summer you feel the bite of autumn and whilst it's beautiful colours dance around you like falling leaves, you miss the dew.

You'll miss the spring in your step and April showers followed by rainbows and you are completely aware that soon your best memories are seasons away.

Cherish the spring, find joy in its misty mornings and grey afternoons because whilst summer is warm it is fleeting.

And in autumn you fear Jack Frost nipping at your nose and making the ground unsteady beneath your once anchored feet on freshly mown grass.

But for now we are vibrant blossoms and lush greenery and long sunlit days. We are spring and summer.

Moonlight

We are drenched in moonlight and covered in
darkness and snuggled together as one.
We are restless but still, tired but awake, old and
new.
A milk soaked smile and a sleepy kind face
huddled in the corner of the room, hiding away
from the distraction of sleep.
The world has switched off. It is you and I.
We are learning.
We are surviving.
And as the sunlight filters through cracks in the
curtains and the new day creeps in, we close our
eyes.
We steal dreams while the world awakens. My
baby and I.

Blanket

I'll follow you through darkness though i hope it
never comes to that.

I'll build bridges and scale buildings to make
sure you're safe.

Not just from obvious dangers. I want to shelter
you from every niggling doubt, from every
unpleasant thought, from every unkind word.

I want you to wear my love like a blanket and
drench yourself in its warmth. I want to be your
in case of emergency, even when you are grown
and if you ever need me I want to be there like I
am now, when you fall and need to be held.

I never want you to feel as though you haven't a
friend in the world, because my baby, I am more
than just your mama. I am your biggest
cheerleader and I would move mountains and
part oceans just sit by your side.

And though I pray it will never happen, I will
follow you through the darkness, just to be your
torch.

Remember

You will never be as little as you are today.
The time just won't stand still.
I study your face each freckle and dimple,
Just trying to get my fill.

Tomorrow you may have grown so tall,
The years might have flown by,
And you might not need your mama,
Because it's your turn to fly.

So today I embrace every tantrum,
Every laugh babble play,
So when its time for you to grow up,
I can remember you like this every day.